# Sharks

# Sharks

## Gary Lopez

THE CHILD'S WORLD®, INC.

Published in the United States of America by The Child's World®, Inc.
PO Box 326
Chanhassen, MN 55317-0326
800-599-READ
www.childsworld.com


**Product Manager** Mary Berendes
**Editor** Katherine Stevenson
**Designer** Mary Berendes
**Contributor** Bob Temple


**Photo Credits**
ANIMALS ANIMALS © Leonard L. T. Rhodes: 23 (main photo)
ANIMALS ANIMALS © Michele Westmorland: 24
ANIMALS ANIMALS © Rudolf Ingo Riepl: 19
© 2001 Brandon D. Cole: 9
© Eiichi Kurasawa, The National Audubon Society Collection/Photo Researchers: 2
© Fred McConnaughey, The National Audubon Society Collection/Photo Researchers: 26
© Jeffrey L. Rotman: cover, 13, 15, 20, 23 (small photo)
© Jonathan Bird/www.oceanicresearch.org: 30
© 1997 Marilyn Kazmers/Dembinsky Photo Assoc. Inc.: 16
© Marilyn & Maris Kazmers/Sharksong: 29
© Tom Campbell/Art Womack Photography: 6, 10

**Library of Congress Cataloging-in-Publication Data**
Lopez, Gary.
Sharks / by Gary Lopez.
p. cm.
Summary: Describes the physical characteristics, behavior, habitat,
and life cycle of sharks and discusses how dangerous they really are.
ISBN 1-56766-614-0 (lib. bdg. : alk. paper)
1. Sharks—Juvenile literature. [1. Sharks.]  I. Title.
QL638.9 .L63 2000
597.3—dc21
99-039014

# On the cover...

Front cover: This sand tiger shark is swimming at night off the North Carolina coast.
Page 2: This large group of hammerhead sharks is swimming off the coast of Japan.

# Table of Contents

The ocean water is clear and blue in the bright sunshine. Under the surface, schools of colorful fish swim through the water. Among them swims a sleek animal with a long tail and very sharp teeth. This animal is cruising through the water looking for its next meal. People all over the world fear this creature. What is it? It's a shark!

⇐ This Caribbean reef shark is swimming
slowly as it searches for food.

## What Do Sharks Look Like?

Sharks belong to the same animal family as fish. They have a long, round body and a powerful tail. On their sides, sharks have two **fins** that help them change directions as they swim. On the sides of their heads, sharks have a number of slits called **gills.** The sharks use their gills to breathe.

Sharks have very rough skin. In fact, many people say that it feels like sandpaper. A shark's skin is rough because it is made up of thousands of tiny **scales,** much like a snake's.

From close up, you can see the roughness ⇒ of this epaulette shark's skin.

Most sharks also have dozens of sharp teeth. These teeth help the shark hold on to the slippery foods it eats. As long as the shark lives, its teeth keep growing. When one tooth breaks or falls out, another grows in its place.

Not all sharks have teeth, though. *Whale sharks* and *basking sharks* are huge animals. Instead of teeth, their mouths are lined with small filters. They eat by opening their large mouths and swimming slowly through the water. Tiny animals called **plankton** wash in and get trapped in the filters, giving the sharks their meal.

⇐ Here divers swim next to a whale shark as it feeds on plankton. The fish in front of the shark's mouth are also eating plankton. They swim just far enough ahead of the shark to keep from being swallowed by mistake.

# Are There Different Kinds of Sharks?

There are hundreds of different kinds of sharks. Some sharks, such as the *mako shark* or the *tiger shark,* can grow to be fairly large. Most sharks, however, are small. In fact, half of all shark types don't even grow to be as long as a baseball bat! Many of these small sharks live on the seafloor in shallow water. They eat things such as shrimp and worms buried in the sand.

This large tiger shark is swimming in the Red Sea. ⇒

## Are Sharks Dangerous?

Smaller sharks are fairly gentle animals. Even many of the larger types are harmless. But some types of sharks can be very dangerous. The *great white shark* is one shark that should be left alone. It can grow to be 20 feet long and weigh almost 3,000 pounds! It has very powerful jaws and hundreds of sharp teeth. Great white sharks eat bigger animals such as seals, sea lions, and dolphins.

This huge great white is swimming near Australia's Dangerous Reef. ⇒

Sharks are most dangerous when they are hungry, bothered, or scared. When this happens, sharks can sometimes attack people. Many shark attacks probably happen when the shark mistakes a person for one of its usual foods. Unlike what you see in scary movies, sharks don't set out to hunt people. Most of the time, they stay far away from people.

⇐ This blue shark was curious about the photographer. As it got closer, the shark became frightened. Here it is quickly turning around to swim away.

## How Do Sharks Hunt?

Sharks find their food by using all their senses. They use their keen sense of smell to find food that is far away. By feeling tiny movements, or **vibrations,** in the water, sharks can tell right where the animal is. As they get closer, sharks can smell and taste the "flavor" of the animal in the water. They can also see their victim, or **prey,** as it swims along.

This grey reef shark is eating a large fish called a grouper.  ⇒

Small and big sharks have different ways of catching their prey. Small sharks slowly sneak up on their prey and then quickly gulp it down. Bigger sharks must work harder for their meals. When a big shark is ready to eat, it circles around its prey. It must be careful not to scare the animal. When it is close enough, the shark swims under the animal and quickly attacks it, biting down with its sharp teeth.

⇐ This great white is attacking bait that was thrown into the water near Australia's Dangerous Reef.

## What Are Baby Sharks Like?

Different kinds of sharks have their babies, or **pups,** in different ways. Most sharks give birth to babies that can swim just as soon as they are born. Others lay eggs that attach to rocks and weeds. From the moment they hatch or are born, shark pups must live on their own. They learn to eat and stay safe all by themselves. Like most other animals, shark pups look just like their parents, only smaller.

*Main photo:* This horn shark egg washed up on a California beach. ⇒
*Small photo:* This young spiny dogfish still has its yolk sac attached after hatching from its egg.

Sharks are very important animals. By eating other animals, sharks help keep the oceans healthy. They eat weak or sick animals, leaving the healthy ones more room to eat and live. Without sharks and other **predators,** our oceans would be overflowing with animals, and many of them would be sick.

⇐ This great white is swimming just under the surface near South Africa's coast.

Sharks have few natural enemies in their ocean world. In fact, sharks' biggest enemy is people. People throughout the world kill sharks to eat or sell their meat and fins. Some people who fish for a living kill sharks because they eat other fish. Sharks also die when they get caught in fishing nets by mistake.

← This scalloped hammerhead shark died after getting caught in a net off Mexico's coast.

## Can We Learn More About Sharks?

Although we have learned a lot about sharks, there is still a lot we do not know. Some types of sharks swim in very deep water, and we know very little about how they live. Scientists still have questions even about the sharks we see all the time. To answer these questions, the scientists are studying all they can about sharks. They learn from sharks kept in zoos. They also learn about sharks by swimming with them—with lots of safety equipment, of course!

Here a scientist is examining a lemon shark in the Bahamas. ⇒

Sharks are some of nature's most interesting animals. Sadly, most people don't understand them. Instead of learning more about sharks, many people are simply afraid of them. But for anyone interested in sharks, there are still plenty of mysteries to be solved!

← The sun lights up this great white's back
as it swims beneath the ocean's surface.

# Glossary

**fins (FINZ)**
Fins are the flaps on a fish's body that help it change directions when swimming. A shark has fins on the sides and top of its body.

**gills (GILZ)**
Sharks breathe through thin slits called gills. As water passes over the gills, air gets trapped and enters the shark's body.

**plankton (PLANK-tun)**
Plankton are very tiny animals that live in the ocean. Some sharks eat plankton.

**predators (PRED-eh-terz)**
Predators are animals that hunt and kill other animals. Sharks are predators.

**prey (PRAY)**
Prey animals are hunted and eaten by other animals. Many sea creatures are prey for sharks.

**pups (PUPS)**
Baby sharks are called pups. Shark pups must fend for themselves from the time they are born.

**scales (SKAYLZ)**
Scales are small, hard plates that cover some animals' skins. Sharks have scales, and so do snakes.

**vibrations (vy-BRAY-shunz)**
Vibrations are tiny movements. Sharks hunt by sensing vibrations in the water.

# Web Sites

http://www.discovery.com/stories/nature/sharkweek/sharkweek.html

http://www.nationalgeographic.com/features/97/sharks/index.html

http://www.pbs.org/wgbh/nova/sharks

http://www.aqua.org/animals/species/sharks.html

http://oceanlink.island.net/aquafacts/sharks.html

# Index